Yaweezy

Yaweezy

Did this really happen

Dorothy Hendrix

iUniverse, Inc.
Bloomington

Yaweezy
Did this really happen

iUniverse books may be ordered through booksellers or by contacting:

iUniverse
1663 Liberty Drive
Bloomington, IN 47403
www.iuniverse.com
1-800-Authors (1-800-288-4677)

ISBN: 978-1-4759-6663-3 (sc)
ISBN: 978-1-4759-6664-0 (ebk)

Printed in the United States of America

iUniverse rev. date: 12/18/2012

Contents

Introduction

A few days ago I realized that my story had reached denouement. My persona wears no masks. My super ego of social restraints has been greatly lightened. The constructs in my egos have come together and the libido of my archetypes feels like rushing wind. Anima and animus working together along with my auto serve effective force (God in me) has guided me through this year from desiring to tell my story up to today when I talked to a publisher's representative at I Universe. They will copyright and ISBN distribute. I am experiencing a little inflation right now. Acting as if has brought me to the realization of a dream that seemed impossible.

I met Jacob at the senior center and he has become my friend and someone to help me with the things that are impossible for me like keeping my printer going and he allows me to hug him and draw energy from his abundant life force.

Since January of this year 2012 to be able to present my story I have had to learn to use my laptop, learn some songs for CDs, some Spanish, some guitar and now how to pull a manuscript together.

I talked to my Spanish teacher today and this is what I told him about where I feel like I am in the process.

"Hey sweetheart, I want to tell you that Jacob did not de-friend me. Someone else did and since then has blocked me from him. I contacted him at his business and he is still willing to help me. Someone does not like what I am writing because I have drawn him into my story. Seems to me like few are open-minded today. I cannot find fault with whoever blocked us when even Mike asked me not to write anything that would get me arrested."

He asked "What do folks need to be more open-minded about?"

I think that a challenge I made to church leaders may have bothered someone and Jacob might be under pressure just by being my friend.

He came back "Can you explain? I am open-minded."

"I am writing about archetypes and God being an archetype of wholeness in us. I think I have broken a taboo."

"I do not see why anyone would object to what you are writing."

My whole life story is based on God working in us as a force that is somehow able to go out into the world of atoms and make real our prayers and dreams. It is about me believing in a down to Earth God as a force within us.

My wise teacher responded "If I am not mistaken what you are saying is keep a positive attitude and believe what you want to achieve so much that in the end it happens. You visualize what you want and work hard to achieve it while staying relaxed and focused. Am I right? This is taught to athletes."

"You are the only one that seems to get it. I have read that our thoughts act as an autoserve mechanism. I call it God."

With a quick response "But this does not rule out anything about there being a God in Heaven or say anything about religion does it?"

"No I just believe that Heaven starts now. Do you suppose that not many people have read anything about this?"

"This is taught in my career classes a lot."

"Well you seem to be the only one that grasps what I am talking about."

I believe that it goes hand in hand with religion. Using my own life as an example I believe I was guided to this time and place for a reason. It has taken me ten years. I stayed focused even when I could not figure things out and finally I began to understand. The timing is where God comes in. The reason that some might not understand this is because they do not understand psychology nor do they understand that they use this type of mindset every day of their lives. Another thing is that some churches teach that if we believe in God everything will be all right. Our faith is in God and the works we do to achieve our goals is where we use our brain. The problem is that most people only have a basic knowledge of the Bible and they frown upon anything like psychology.

With all that said, I will go back to January 24, 2012 when Jacob came. I was anxious to the point of eating a whole foot long and a bag of cookies. Then a voice came to me from the universal subconscious found in books. "Remember that God works on analog and on digital." Like a heat seeking missile my immediate needs are met by my brain power. If I don't know what I need, then one thought leads to another or one action leads to another until my needs are met. To me this is virtual reality.

The particular need that I have right now is to program a social network. I want to write my life story. Thinking about this I remembered Jacob. He works at the senior center just down the street and he teaches computer. I called and he made time for me that day after work.

God is not a mystery to me. My auto serve is built into me and it is the energy of the universe, but right now I am thinking about how to raise my consciousness to a Nibiruan level.

For years while a lot of folks were reading Star Wars, I have been reading books about Nibiru. This author is an interpreter of the dead languages and especially Sumerian. As I understand it Nibiru is a rogue planet with a 3,600 year orbit. According to the Sumerians it will perogee in the asteroid belt sometime soon.

This planet is supposed to place protection between earth and the sun and help our planet with ascension. It may be Planet X that is being discussed today. One author spent his whole career studying this and believed the text so much that he even registered Nibiru at NASA as the next sighted planet. I have read all his books and they are food for thought but what I want is space age consciousness. To me Nibiru is a symbol of a virtual reality where we are not limited to this dimension.

Our Bible speaks of the 3rd heaven and is full of heavenly chariots. What if consciousness is a starship and our pineal gland is a stargate? Could we teleport thru the 4th dimension of spacetime, the 5th penteract, the 6th of hexaract, the 7th of superstrings, the 8th of trancendence, then all the way to ascenscion of time travel?

I believe that we do travel with our imaginations. We only limit ourselves. A book I read often calls it the inner reaches of outer space. One website I enjoyed has now been discontinued. It had a song about Nibiru. I jotted down the words and recorded the music from a song called "Paint the sky with stars." The lyrics are haunting and often possess many different meanings. I think that one meaning could be that in times of darkness you must find things that lighten your burdens. This song can be found easily on the Internet using "Paint the sky with stars lyrics" as a search if you would like to hear it.

I like to think that we do live in virtual reality and our consciousness is ascending in accelerated time.

It is 2012 and here in Wilmington KY everyone is living in the fast lane. It is hard to settle down and write but I am seventy eight years old and I think my story is worth telling. I have written a prayer book for two of my grandchildren but this is my philosophy of why I have been able to enjoy my life in spite of the turmoil going on around me.

As my catch line I want you to know that this first part of my story is true and it is about a Columbian Brujo by the name of Salvadore. It is about how this medicine man led me to enter altered states where I was enabled to perceive other dimensions without drugs. He taught me a form of self-hypnosis.

When I was thirty two years old I daydreamed a lot. One day a friend that worked for the telephone company came by for coffee and told me that the Pioneers were getting together a group to go to Paris. Mike, my husband, knew that it was a dream of mine and he said "Let's do it."

When I was a little girl my brother called me either Madame Pompadour or Miss Astor because he said that I was always determined to have my way. Now knowing that I would be in Paris I began to read French history and had a friend sketch a picture of me sitting on the Moon and another friend photographed it.

The next thing I knew Mike and I were boarding Delta. We had been living on prayer for a long time and had to borrow the money to go and we had five children we had to be here for. The perfect solution came about. I believe that one author called it synchronicity. It began to be serendipity as soon as we stepped on the plane at Atlanta. The airline had sold our seats and they were occupied. The hostess ushered us to first class because that was all that was available. There we were, munching on fillets and sipping wine for the same price we had already paid.

I had gone through several sad years between the divorce from my first husband and marrying Mike. During that time I had what I called a journey into fullness. I studied the Bible and power of positive thinking. In fact I read everything I could to try and move forward in life. I have read that "You will see it when you believe it." I worked hard on my beliefs and prepared myself for miracles. Mike was sent from above to help me with my children and now I was strolling down the Champs Elysees, stepping into a little café for a sip of new beaujolais and fresh fruit from Brittany.

Was this really me at the Lourve looking at the Winged Victory and The Mona Lisa? I had caviar at LaBelle France way up at the Eiffel Tower and toured Port d' Versaille. We went over the pass into the French Alps and stood at the top of Mt. Blanc and looked down at the Glacier. I took pictures in Provence, Annecy and Lyon, pictures of lavender fields and sunflower fields. We saw castles and so many things that my whole world seemed larger.

I had taken a picture of a troubador in front of the Pope's Palace and on the flight home I was thinking that I needed some art lessons before I painted him. Then another thought came to me that if I learned more about portrait painting I might even like to illustrate. I nudged Mike and asked him what he thought about me taking some classes in the fall semester.

Continuing Education gave me the opportunity to take acrylics (from the head of the Art Department who was a friend) and creative writing.

There were two creative writing teachers-John and Cindy-a husband and wife team. They were inspiring to me from the very first day. Mike and I still had our youngest son at home and I still cooked three meals a day but writing and painting were always on my mind.

John and Cindy told the class to experience emotionally as we recorded our thoughts even if we were sure we would end up in the fiery pit. My upbringing in the church, fear of offending the family, the voices of those that had controlled me and most of all my own censorship began to fade.

We were given ideas to develop and I began to see that all the reading I had done in my lifetime was not in vain. One of the ideas was "You are driving along a back road and you see a book in the road with its' pages fluttering in the wind."

My first thought was that I wanted to see why anyone would leave a book to ruin and what the book was about. I stopped and went back for it but when I reached to pick it up it was no longer there. A woman stood in the spot holding the book out to me as she spoke quietly. "I am Ouanita and this should help you." I took the book and saw the title was about the flight of the feathered serpent. I experienced a brief stream of consciousness triggered probably by the books I had recently been reading about Quetzalcoatl and Astrology. In my mind's eye the book was about Salvadore the Columbian Brujo who would be my guide.

After that semester I put my notes into a drawer, planning one day to develop them. Now Jacob was coming to give me some private lessons on how to use the computer so I could write my story and give it to the world. I had purchased my laptop in September of 2010 but circumstances did not allow me either the time or peace of mind to pursue anything.

On the 24th of October, 2010 Mike's youngest son Brandon was killed by two doctors. I had the experience of being a second mother to Brandon from the time he was four years old and when he died he was forty six. Brandon and I had formed a bond from working and praying and spending a lot of time together. I will not go into the medical reason for his death because I do not know how. The death certificate stated accident. One doctor did a heartburn and over corrected and blood was leaking into his lungs, at least a half pint. He could not breathe so another doctor ordered a balloon in his throat and punctured an artery, which led to liters of blood leaking into his lungs. Brandon seized and died. It was months before Mike and I could think straight.

Going back further to 2006 I had serious surgery at M.D. Anderson and in 2008 a knee replacement. Somewhere in between I had to be put on a chemical rest for six months to correct an imbalance brought on by too much medication and worry. Finally now in January of 2012 I find myself mentally alert enough to use the computer. I called Jacob to help me learn computer because I had met him at our senior center where he was filling in as a basic computer instructor. I was impressed with the way he treated me then, still am and always will be.

I lived and functioned during all that time from September 2010 until now and wrote a blog trying to understand my purpose. I could use the word processor but now I wanted to tell my story. I thought my blog was for the purpose of telling my story but I have not seen anyone but me that has used it this way.

I seem to be skipping and jumping but going back and remembering and pulling together a coherent story is a challenge. I am going to tell a little about what I blogged to set the stage.

Romancing the Stone

I called my blog Romancing the Stone because the White Stone in Revelation has been in my sight every day and in everything I have done for forty years or more. The White Stone is the cube that unfolds into a cross when we have reached the highest degree of consciousness we are capable of attaining.

So I began my blog with Salvadore, my Columbian shaman that had been tucked in a drawer for years.

You see, something of this nature really happened to me back in 1987. Three friends and I decided to go to Little Rock to visit a psychic by the name of Ouanita St. John. She spent the whole day with us and her readings for my friends were terrible but accurate for it all has come to pass.

One friend was predicted to endure a horrible divorce. Another friend was going to have arterial disease and she has since had a stroke and been bedridden for ten years. She told the third friend she would raise another child which she did.

By the time she got to me I was ready to run. She looked me square in the eyes and said "You have an angel on your right shoulder and he is a German professor that will be your life long teacher."

My daughter was a Reference librarian and within the week she called me to say that she had a large box of books donated by a man who said he would like for the right person to have them. Knowing that all books are my joy she called and asked me if I wanted them. Imagine my shock when the first nineteen books were by Carl Jung as translated by Hull. This seemed pretty close to a German professor to me. In addition there were texts by Joseph Campbell, Edgar Cayce, Jane Roberts and Carlos Castaneda. There were books on hypnosis, psychology, psycho cybernetics, Mayan astrology, Kabbalah and some work books as well.

The man that donated the books said they had belonged to his son who had recently died. Now I had been given this gift from the Universal Subconscious mind of all these writers of Consciousness. So in my mind's eye as I looked at the title of the book the woman stood holding out to me I created Salvadore, another part of my personality. I had been listening to the voices of all these authors of Psyche and now I was ready to channel Sal. I may write at another time about all the Columbian mysteries Sal shared with me.

My story now is about my Christian Journey. As with every story beginning there was and is the word. I had heard a lot of fire and brimstone and prayed without ceasing most of my life but never read the Bible. Then in 1963 my first husband left me and my three children. I hurt so much that I began a search for purpose in my Bible. It would be 1983 and more pain before I finally became so desperate that I went to a Charismatic prayer meeting where the veil of my mind was split and lifted. I began to eat the scripture, comparing verse to verse.

I found myself taking a symbolic journey out of bondage from a sin poor Eve committed through a bloody old covenant and eventually to a new covenant where Jesus poured His blood once and for all over the Arc of the Covenant as a symbol that we are under a new Covenant of love. This is all a symbolic journey through Hebrew history that we as Christians take just to understand why Christ (or the anointing) lives in us.

The path I followed through the wilderness of my soul in the scriptures was Salvation, Justification, Baptism, Sanctification, Glorification, the Anointing and etc.

I came to understand that the Stone with the new name in Revelation was just me and everyone on their journey into Fullness.

I finally came to the understanding that we are all Israel, just different tribes.

Why the church leaders have hoarded this information has got to be power. There is no church if there is no Immaculate Conception, no Crucifixion, no Resurrection, no Heaven except in us just where Jesus said it would be. It's all a symbolical journey of our psyche. Recently more people have begun to know that we did not have to go through so much fear and helplessness. Our church leaders either did not know that the Bible is history and symbol or they withheld all they knew for their own gain.

I consider myself one of the most blessed because I learned to hear the voices from the Bible as well as the voices from the Universal Consciousness of Jung and others. I learned about my personality development, the symbols of transformation, the voices within of my ego, persona, shadow, anima, animus and mostly of my own true self. I learned about myth, Kabbalah, my nervous system and separate realities and dimensions.

Nothing can come out of my mind that I have not first put in. As I have studied all the wonderful writers that have gone before me I channel their voices from the Cosmos. I have so many books to learn from that I will never be able to touch the surfaces of all of them. Every time I sit down with one of them I enter a heightened state where I perceive other worlds.

All my reading helped me to know that I generate God in myself. God is a symbol for wholeness. God lives in my brain as my autoserve and is working all things for my good.

We may be preprogrammed with our purpose in our DNA, which we then find or not. There is something bigger than anyone has yet to understand that we may also call God that holds everything together. For me it is enough right now to know that God serves me. I don't have to make brownie points for Heaven.

How simple yet how complicated we are made. We program this energy with our own thinking. When things go wrong we need to examine our thoughts. This God energy we hold does not ask why we want something. The undirected energy hears our direction and does it, good or bad. That is free will.

When we dream we intend and wonderful things happen like magic. Even before I completely grasped the magnitude I asked for the wonderful experience of going to Europe.

A synopsis of what I wanted to put on paper for my own satisfaction of mind at this point of my blog would be to say I am no longer under bondage to a set of dogmas that our church leaders have held us hostage to for over two thousand years.

Oh I listen to the voices from the Bible and these voices tell me we are Gods, creating our own personal reality.

Raising our consciousness is what we have been doing all our lives unless we have had terminal brainlock.

Alchemy is about changing base metal into gold but is really a symbol for changing our base nature which we have to do ourselves.

So sure intuitively I am right, I have been falsely programmed to doubt myself all my life.

My children are not even remotely interested in my life but every now and then I try to tell them a bit about how exciting my days are. I really want them to confirm that I am on track. In response to one of these attempts my daughter said "Mother you might need to define some of those terms you use because I don't have a clue to what you are saying." One of my sons said "Mom I don't believe most of us are conscious enough yet to believe that we are gods."

This is the sad part. I did not understand all of this myself when they were children or I might have been able to teach them.

John 10:31-36 tells how the people wanted to stone Jesus for telling them they were gods. I have never heard a preacher give a sermon on this and I had to find it for myself.

As for my daughter, she has a good point. From my point of view my ego is conscious and is everything I have ever learned. My persona is how I act in this world. Below my conscious level but on the job day and night is my shadow(repressed material). My shadow is making conscious those things that my ego is ready to safely integrate. My anima is my feminine intuition and my animus is my masculine aggressive nature that goes out into the world to accomplish my heart's desire.

This is the mystic marriage or chemical wedding that must take place within us and outwardly in our world. It is masculine and feminine energy working together.

It is possible to change our brain chemicals and to a certain extent even our brain circuits by taking control of our thoughts and emotions. The chemical wedding is Christ's consciousness or Nibiru's consciousness ascending. We generate God within to the degree we desire.

There are two sides to everything and up to this point I have been writing about spirit. Now my thoughts turn very physical.

How passionate is my art with its' terrifying consequence. The part of my brain that gives me courage to express myself, excitement and panic and even anger. The desire for hot blooded coupling, emotion laden cravings, lustful drives from frustration and loneliness. A magnificent personal symphony, unbridled and out of control. Only my self consciousness tempers all the yearnings of my heart. If I dare to reveal my passions and allow you to look into the mirror of my soul will you be overcome with desire to restore my trust in love that others stole.

Suckle the rings of color on my breast
Cup the petals of my labia
And suffer with me the pain
As you enter the threshold
Be the one to stay with me
Let me give myself not in vain
Lightening joins earth to heaven
My passionate art expressed
Shaking pillars of the sky
My explosive quest
There is nothing quite like the feeling
Being alive and sharing a love
Like the Aurorae Borealis
Across the Northern skies above
The hardness of his body
Caresses like the wild Gulf breeze
His muscles hold mysteries
That only I can read
Stormy days and Sundays
Are joyous times of rest
Romping and playing like little ones
Our oneness uniquely expressed
His lips roll the clouds back
Give me wings to fly
Just do it, don't ask why

There is nothing like the feeling
Of being alive and sharing a love
Like the Aurora Borealis
Across the Northern skies above

Around this time I discovered that a social network was coming out with a place to write our stories. When I bought my laptop in September 2010 the salesperson programmed the page for me but I had not understood how posts could help me. Now I could have a whole wall to create my life story so I began to pray how to go about starting this process. As I wrote at the beginning, I thought of Jacob and asked him if he would help me.

I need to digress again here and insert a little bit of a sad situation that happened over an undetermined period of time to one of my granddaughters. She had been unhappy for some time and finally resorted to cutting herself to ease her pain. She ran away, she said, because her stepdad had been abusing her. I was worried about a situation that all I could do was pray about but she ended up taking her puppy and going to live with her dad.

Soon she met and married a serviceman and now they are having a baby. The main reason I wanted to use the social network was to write my story but I was also very excited that I could album my great grandchild from birth.

Now I will go back to the beginning of this story from when I called Jacob to see if he could give me computer lessons at my home. He came that day.

Over the next few months as Jacob worked with me I began to think of him as the tall, dark, silent one because he never disclosed anything.

However at that first lesson I ranted about how I had to hurry and learn before the baby was born. When he realized who I was talking about it hit him like a ton bricks and before he thought he said "We wondered what happened to her." Then it came out that he went to the church that was pastored by the father of a friend she had spent so much time with while she was troubled.

We did not talk about it anymore but I did marvel at the coincidence and briefly wondered how well he knew her and if he knew of all her heartaches. I believe I told him that she had escaped a cyclone of destruction when she left this town.

Jacob taught me a lot at each lesson and I started writing the continuation of my thoughts. I prayed and studied and accepted intellectually that I was free from all the lies I had been taught by those that had tried to control me for their own purposes.

I know that God is living undirected energy within me available for me to program and my only limits were the ones I put on myself.

The rut of doubt still ran something like this: what if you are wrong?

I had been reading a book about the bicameral and unicameral mind and it brought to my conscious thinking a statement that I read somewhere that really struck a chord.

"Man' insanity might sometimes be Heaven' sense."

I am still studying how my mind works. Hearing all the legion of voices through books was a natural process to me because my Mom heard voices. I was just three months old when my Mother developed schizophrenia. It was right after the depression and my grandmother told me that times were so lean that my mother ate the crumbs if my two brothers left any. Grandmother said she always tried to send a pan of biscuits to the little cabin my father provided for us.

My uncle, Mother's brother, came to the little house to bring us a pan of biscuits. Mother was sitting on the steps with me in one arm and balancing her Bible in her other hand. Mother laid the Bible down and smiling through tears said "Brother I am Jesus."

The next thing that happened was the police were taking her across the state line to a mental hospital. Grandmother never said that there had been any other episodes that scared everyone but fear of the different had taken over.

Moving away from my story for a minute I want to tell about something my son told us while eating lunch with us a few days ago.

He said that a friend of his had eye surgery and the Doctor put him on steroids. He began to tell people that he was God. He was sent to a local addiction recovery clinic. I told him that the steroids probably activated a neurotransmitter that fit a synapse and that gave him the powerful feeling and that we are gods.

Back to my mother's story, what she read in the Bible caused her ego boundaries to collapse and she understood who she was. Maybe her brain organization had reverted to the bicameral state that I understand Mankind existed in right up to the time of the Iliad.

In this day and time our central nervous system is unicameral. The two legislative chambers of our brain work together and make conscious what we need to understand. We have discernment.

I have also read that during the bicameral time of evolution our left side generated ideas and commands and our right obeyed blindly. During that period the voices from the left hemisphere were gods and demons. One author feels that schizophrenia might be a throwback to the bicameral involving neurotransmitters and maybe the Reticular Activating System.

My ego boundaries collapsed in 1982. At that time it seemed to me I had lost all control of my life. Just as I have done all my adult life I reached for my Bible. Sure enough there it was just as Mother had read,

"It is not I that liveth but Christ that liveth in me."

Jesus, or Christ, is a metaphor for the archetype of the awakening in our consciousness that we are anointed.

By divine guidance, Scott Peck's book "The Road Less Traveled" was given to me at this time. Taking in his knowledge allowed me to suspend my disbelief and hear my own voice of innocence from a time when I did not feel responsible for everyone.

I had learned from Norman Vincent Peale and Smiley Blanton back when my first husband left our family that no matter where a person is in their journey someone else has gone through pretty much the same thing and written about it.

When we take in their message the left side of our brain sends symbols of transformation to the right side and our unicameral brain which works through our nervous system sends information to our body, mind and more. We experience a flash of knowledge or perhaps healing. One book calls this action our auto serve mechanism of God's energy in us. This book convinced me that the energy produced by the two hemispheres or our brain acting together actually goes out into the Universal Subconscious and by the law of attraction brings us our heart's desires.

Even my family Doctor tells me that there is first our thought, then gestation or dwelling on it which moves us to action.

I have always pursued every avenue I felt could move me forward and during all this study my Pastor offered a class on Bible as History and Symbol. I sat in that class several Sundays and it reestablished the covered symbols that my journey into fullness had already used to set me free from a bunch of Hebrew laws.

The hard part of just living out our dreams is getting up off our butts and starting. Once started, one thing will lead to another and soon our goal is reached. If we do not know our goal but grasp every opportunity that is put in our path, we are being led by the desires of our hearts and like the magic of my trip to Europe we find unexpected pleasures.

I knew I wanted to tell my story of how absolutely charmed my life had been but I had no outline. I just began to write what I heard in my mind. I was trying to turn the energy of my thoughts into words.

Remembering or musing about all I had written so far I thought about how I had experienced altered states since I was five years old.

Once I went to the altar to pray, desperate for answers, and suddenly I was praying in tongues. I believe it is self-hypnosis brought on by the music and my own programming releasing endorphins and the latent language part of our brain.

It seemed to scare everyone except the Deaf Minister who came and knelt with me.

It made me laugh to think of how a lot of folks don't understand some of my actions and honestly I think I like to shock sometimes,

For instance, several months ago one of our Sunday School teachers was concerned that Mike and I had not attended for a while. He urged us to come the next Sunday because he was going to teach the Trinity. Then he told us that he had been diagnosed as having an aneurism in his brain stem.

Sometimes a good scare will cure hiccups so my left hemisphere thought. Since I have had the benefit of learning that we are all Christ, I will demonstrate the Trinity and maybe just the daring of it might work a miracle.

We don't know the extent of our power and if we never try to use it then we will never know. My whole life has been one of spiritual experiment so this time I knew I would shock the class and my teacher. The Church Literature had only that Sunday given up the fact that we are all Christ, or anointed.

I have no trouble with boldness or rejection because I have had to deal with them both more times than I care to remember.

At the right time during the class I asked to speak. My teacher said "As long as it doesn't involve me."

I went to him, placed my hands on his neck and explained that the Trinity is will, wisdom and action. I commanded the aneurism dissolved and his brain sound and in order. He is still alive and had no surgery. I never mentioned what I did. It has never been mentioned again.

I am writing about these instances of altered states and leaps of faith to prepare your minds and hearts for the things that will happen to me now as my story unfolds surprising even me!

Our other Sunday School teacher's son Drew was a music major and at one time his lung collapsed and the class had sent a lot of loving thoughts his way. Drew is doing fine now.

By now Jacob had me established on the social network and was teaching me how to navigate a little deeper.

Drew created a group for his fans and I tried to encourage him but did not know what to say. I posted that my musical education was not up to par but I would love to follow as best as I could. One night Mike and I went to hear him play and sing. He sang jazz and oldies like "A Nightingale Sang in Berkley Square." Somehow this brought memories of all the mother figures that had shaped me.

I want to tell how Drew's nightingale song inspired me to write "The Voices of the Nightingales." We don't go out at night much anymore. The lights are like Carnivale and the ground wants to come up and meet me. This once I begged Mike to take me to Genusa's supper club just for a few minutes because I wanted the experience of hearing Drew sing in the ambiance of the little piano bar.

We staggered in and sat at the bar. All the tables were taken. I ordered champagne and chocolate pie. The waitress made it special by topping my glass with raspberry liqueur. I sipped my drink and projected my excitement on the whole scene. When Drew sang "A Nightingale Sang in Berkley Square" it was like a caress from yesterday. A nightingale seems to be like a much sought for whisper. On the way home I began to hear voices of the mothers of my life whispering their stories like nightingales in chorus.

My first mother was my grandmother, my mothers' mother. She was a strong woman and worked on the 40 acre farm where she and Grandpa lived. I was born in 1934 when the Depression was just ending and all of their five children had made homes of their own. As I wrote before my mother had developed schizophrenia and was back and forth from the hospital for years. Grandpa and Grandma kept me with them for seventeen years.

Mike's mother had already entered her rest when I met her. She birthed eleven children including a set of twins. Her back had given out so she rocked in her special chair and often said "I have the greatest children in the world." At that time I could not see that she was looking through to a time when life had buffed them and God had become their center. I could see peacefulness in her eyes.

Then there was Granny Nightingale, my first husband's mother. She did not ask for me but I married her son and she made herself a teacher to us for eleven years. She was sort of Florence Nightingale, she sacrificed. She made melt-in-your-mouth butter roll pies and taught me how to cook and sew. If there was one fig she gave it to me but she controlled our marriage. It was a love you today stay out of my way tomorrow relationship. She rested by quoting scripture. Her song lingers and I hear her voice every time I pass her picture which I still have hanging in my hall fifty years later.

My mother was a caged nightingale held captive by a disease that was little understood at that time. But she still sang. Somehow God put a tatting shuttle in her hands and gave her a desire to create. She had known freedom before the chemicals in her brain became unbalanced. Then after I was born she just couldn't cope any longer. The rest of her life she sat, first in the hospital, sometimes at Grandma's, and then in a nursing home. She tatted row after row of lace and people would buy a length and she would smile. When she died the nursing home director said "She preached her own funeral every day by her sweet spirit. She had entered her rest."

I can now pinpoint when each one of them entered their rest. I left the farm when I was seventeen and by nineteen had a beautiful baby girl. One day I thought life was not treating me right and so I decided to take my little girl and go back to those acres where life was so peaceful. My wonderful

Grandma sang out loud and clearly "This is not your home anymore." She told me to go and work out my troubles and create my life.

I wasn't real happy about that but I did go back to my home. It was years before I understood that she had entered her rest. When I had lived with them she would take a walk down the country road that lead to the farm every evening. The yard dogs always went with her and Grandpa said that they would protect her from even a bear. That was her time for prayer and rest.

The Bible says that there is a rest from all our worries and anxiety but that many fail to find it because of unbelief. My mothers showed me the way but it took a good long time for me to find it.

I had strong guidance from these women and it has kept me from crumbling totally and urged me to search for truth always.

Drew's dad, George, sent me an Email after he read my posts to Drew and my praise for my mothers.

Talk about altered states, when I read his Email is when this story really begins.

The Prophecy

I opened George's Email and I can say that of all my life's experiences it was the most amazing feeling of déjà vu that swept over me. This was over the top.

He wrote "Don't ever doubt yourself. You are unique on this planet. You don't have to measure up to what you think others are expecting of you. Keep on being the wonderfully unusual person that you are. God loves you just the way you are."

By this time George understood that I was writing my story and since he had known me for over half of my life, he knew that I would write some complicated stuff.

He wrote some other things like take one step at a time and one thing will lead to the next so just stay with the journey and let your light shine.

My subconscious had taken over and was integrating information to my quasi-conscious mind in the form of a newsreel passing in front of my eyes.

I lay on the floor of the local judge's living room and an Evangelist stood over me prophesying. I heard her say "You will laugh, run, sing and dance." There was more but I could not hear her. I was moving away into an existence that had no physical form. The Bible calls it the Circumcision of the Heart.

I knew that all the pain I had ever experienced was being removed from my heart and mind. Now I was reliving the event and my subconscious was bringing the full Prophecy to my remembrance.

A few pages back I told about going to a Charismatic prayer meeting that inspired me to go on the journey into fullness through the Bible. This all had taken place there at that meeting.

I could never in all these years remember what happened until I read the words George wrote.

Somehow my subconscious held it in reserve until now and somehow the words were fed through the universal subconscious to George's conscious mind to give to me. Then it all came back to me. I had stood before the church convention the next day and challenged their decisions to bar charismatics. This was the first message sent through me to the church. "What is the matter with you preachers? What are you afraid of? Don't you believe you are covered by the blood of Christ? Don't be holier than thou, Feed my sheep."

The doubts that I had to this point about my having a need to write my story melted away. In fact I took this as a sign not to doubt whatever I was hearing.

There was and is a greater, unique mystery here, and I am being given the magnificent opportunity to solve it. I think I am probably unique because I do not live entirely in this third dimension. My imagination is a time capsule and I travel wherever I want, either in the past or future or other dimensions.

I have been reading a book about Revelation. At the end of Revelation, the Word says "I am the Alpha and Omega." This suggests that Jesus was the first way shower of a new breed of humans in embryo. These are humans that are fantasy-prone and need magic. They are humans that refuse to live narrow, unfulfilled lives, dictated by others.

When we "act as if," our dreams are already on the way to coming true.

Might we be omega children, taught for brief periods by a higher reality to mold and shape our precognitions and change the world little by little?

One author was destitute when she said she remembered a fantastic character in her mind, and now the whole world craves to experience the magician within themselves.

Using a social network is giving me the chance to "act as if." I create what my brain decodes and interprets as signals from my subconscious.

My days are so filled with various thoughts and now and then I began to wonder how I should go about learning some Spanish songs.

My short time goals for this year were to learn computer, write my story, and sing in Spanish. This seemed so simple but I couldn't do any of this without someone to teach me and some other actors to be with me on this stage I am creating.

I began to recall from my past the reason for my future.

He was a cousin to neighbors who lived down the hill. I sat in our sandy driveway running sand through my fingers and crying.

He walked by, stopped and knelt to ask "Why are you crying little one?" I told him that they buried my dad today. He smiled, cupped my chin and said "It's OK, you don't have to say goodbye, just say so long for now Dad." He put his arm around me ad drew me to his knee. He sang me a Spanish lullaby. There was the familiar sensation of being in a safe place like my father's arms as I lay my head on his shoulder.

Suddenly I was back sitting in the sand and he was walking away. He called over his shoulder "Lay your head in your window every evening and I will sing for you."

He was there for a week and every evening I could clearly hear him singing so I memorized the lullaby.

Many years later I went to the local university and sang it for a student in the Spanish Department. He interpreted it as best he could from the way I had heard it.

"When you are all alone on a starry night under the palm trees the light of the stars will always be a testament of my love for you."

The words lingered at the edge of my mind and comforted me like the song. I knew that one day I would share a Spanish lullaby with someone for some reason.

A time for all things, a time for every purpose under Heaven and I knew the time had come to learn my song.

I enrolled in Spanish class at the senior center. I would now have two teachers from the center. Jacob is still giving me a lesson every few weeks and now Joel would open a new door of joy in my brain.

Synchronicity again. I opened the lid of my piano stool which I hardly ever did because I had to loosen the Velcro and remove the cover. There was no rhyme or reason for it, I just did it.

There in the stool lay a piece of sheet music in Spanish. I had never seen it before.

I started playing the music and my hair bristled like static electricity was running across it.

The words were in Spanish and Googled out as "You are." I felt like new pieces for purpose were falling into place.

I went to four classes at the center and Joel was replaced by a new teacher.

At that last class, in walked a little man that could have been a medicine man. As I have pointed out I live with one foot in this world and the other in Fantasy. I practice self hypnosis to the extent of giving myself commands but have never thought of being hypnotized.

Suddenly this little man grabbed my hands and said "Divide your words into syllables."

Then the student sitting by me punched me and said the class was over.

A few days later I walked by the $5.00 CD bin in a local market and right on top lay a CD by Miredessa of Spanish love songs.

I knew these were the songs.

I called Joel and asked him if he could divide the words of the songs into syllables. He agreed and I got the chords from the internet and begin to learn to play and sing in Spanish.

Jacob was showing me something on the laptop and I was seriously interested.

At some point I realized that we had shifted in our chairs and our thighs were locked against each other. I felt warmth and electricity and I wanted the feeling.

A thought swept over me.

This is the virtue that Jesus said went out from Him when he healed the woman with the issue of blood.

It was confusingly sexual and spiritual and it carried me back to the time when I was five years old and was first aware of a love made possible by the man called Jesus, a father's love.

My next thought was of the man that sang me a Spanish song.

All in a few seconds my first love at sixteen, my first husband's touch and Mike's all seemed to match what I was feeling now.

I wanted to call it virtue but it was pure unadulterated, raw, creative libido. Jacob was absorbed in teaching and never noticed so neither of us moved apart. The feelings were of ecstasy so I just let them happen. I drank them in in large gulps while it lasted. That evening these words came to me:

Our fifth dimensional love
Carries a quintessential control
You touch me in all my secret places
I quiver with delight in my soul

It's my turn now, I'll go slow
Moment by moment my feelings grow
Turn now, enjoy the fire
It roars and hisses, explosions of desire

Are we omega children awakening in a spiritual revolution where for short periods we are allowed into a 5th dimension of virtue where events unfold according to our passions?

Those accusing thoughts that have so often discouraged me said "You are delusional." But I then said "No, there is something very holographic here."

Everything I perceive and feel is a product of my brain decoding signals so that incomprehensible becomes comprehensible.

For some reason I was falling in love with my teacher who was younger that my youngest child.

I had read some in the Kabbalah and this was definitely the rising of the serpent, the spiritual orgasm that was rising from my loins and shooting through my spine and out the top of my head. This was kundalini energy raising my consciousness by sexual stimulation as a creative force. Jacob had reached into my brain and brought new cells to life. My psyche had been nearly numbed for some time by grief and concern but now I was thinking again.

I knew if Jacob sensed my quickening it would change our dynamics and I had already noticed that he was not answering my messages.

I have always seen him as tall, dark and silent because other than teaching he offered no small talk and his messages were guarded.

I figured that knowing as much about computers as he does, he was just careful.

He has a business and family to protect.

He was teaching me a bit about his video editing and my favorite and his was "Lamb of God." I had sent it to my activity log so I could listen without going to his videos.

I noticed that some of my posts to him had disappeared from my log. I thought that someone had deleted them but was not concerned.

I would go to his video and listen because there was a part of him in the video that puzzled me.

The video is about Jesus giving himself as the sacrificial Lamb and somewhere in the music and scenes I began to see Jacob, the man, as mysteriously connected to me. He had responded to my need like magic works.

I began to wonder just who he was and why, when I prayed for teachers, he was sent. I thought about his prayerful connection to my granddaughter.

When he came to teach me and started to leave each time I would hug him. That's nothing new for me, I am a hugger.

In fact a few days ago in a restaurant I was nuzzling on the neck of one of our friends and telling him that I confused another friend.

He gently unwound me from him and said "Live with it girl, you confuse everyone."

With Jacob, he never raised his arms from his side; he just let me love him as long as I wanted without touching me or saying a word. It became as natural to me as hugging anyone I love.

I began working my way through several thought processes. It was as though to my eyes Jacob's appearance changed. I could see the true virtue written in his voice and manner.

I started reading Song of Songs and identified with the Shulamite maiden saying kiss me again and again. Come bring me to your bedroom and etc. Was I destined to repeat a life lesson that had taken place in 2006?

I would scream right now but I'm the only one it would scare. A paddy wagon is all it might bring.

I had made my own rules that year and allowed myself to love my dentist.

I have always had to give my love to someone when I was not receiving love in the romantic way I need. At times Mike would shut me out when he was angry or full of concerns of his own.

It's harmless to anyone and they usually never even know. In my imagination I build someone up to hero status and they are someone I can lean on.

I knew even back then that I was projecting my animus onto them and it is not a harmful process. It's just identifying with the masculine side of myself. It got me though some tough days but I am human enough that I wound up disappointed when in reality he let me down by his own human weakness.

I wrote "Road to Righteousness" for that man and now here I am writing my story and it is partially for Jacob as I project my animus onto him.

One day I saw that Jacob had defriended me. I Emailed him and asked him why.

He wrote three words that became a lifeline for me.

"I did not!"

Then we were totally blocked. There was no other answer. Someone was censoring his mail and blocking me in every direction from him.

I am a seventy eight year old lady just being the person I have always been. I am no threat to a forty two year old that I have found to be a man of honor.

I still had his cell phone number and would message him if I needed him. He was always kind and generous and we just did not discuss his personal life.

I did say to him at one point "Jacob don't forget me." His voice gentled and he said "I won't forget you."

In the meantime I continued learning more about video editing and posting synopsis on different books.

George supported me with an occasional comment until one day I heard within my mind a post that would be like I had slapped him hard.

He has dedicated his whole life to singing in the choir and teaching the Bible.

When the message kept repeating in my thoughts I remembered that in the Prophecy he'd said don't ever doubt yourself.

Let There Be Light

Genesis begins with will, wisdom, and activity hovering over a formless mass and they cried "Let there be Light!"

When I decided to tell my story those same forces were set into motion showing me step by step the way.

I became a cocreator with the power of the Universe.

My story may be small but the same energy is available to me as if I were a well known author.

I was not ready to stop just because the events had turned strange. I was still depending of my effective force to lead me to an unknown finish.

I must have posted a million posts by now and met so many new friends, several band members among them. I thought of their music and of their encouraging support of each other as I hovered and prayed. I posted the message.

"Choirs in churches sing canticles to a dead God while hypnotizing a congregation of wounded people into joining them.

Church leaders are being paid huge salaries while feeding their egos and throwing a few crumbs of a false message to a starving community.

Then they draw the people in so they can drain them of the meager money and time to further the beautiful church.

If I want to cry I will go to church; if I want to laugh I will party with my new musician friends that lift each other up.

Finding a Jesus that has never been lost will not do any good as long as the big secret is hidden from the masses.

God does not live in Heaven unless Heaven lives in us."

After being friends all these years George was not answering my messages. I believe he will one day understand that I had to do it.

This was the denouement I spoke of in my Introduction, the turning point in my story. Jacob and George were not answering my messages.

I have never imposed myself on anyone but I could not give up Jacob as my teacher until I understood whether it was someone blocking him from me or if he was doing it and was just tired of being my friend, too polite to hurt my feelings. After all while I am creating this personal reality play he is creating his own world and merely extending his time to me. It is not my business why the block is there and who is doing it. Besides he is the main character in my play and I'm not nearly to a place where I don't see him.

I had taken all the mind trips of Romancing the Stone, Virtual Reality and dimensions and then, without my introducing it, George gave me the Prophecy. That made me realize that the purpose of my story is really about my search for whatever God energy is. I had felt it so often in my life but coming from Jacob I called it virtue.

Then after one lesson, as Jacob started to leave he came back to my side and put his arm on my shoulder and drew my head to him. There it was again, a blank moment and I felt like I was waking up as he walked away.

Jacob had been the most respectful person I had ever met and even in that small hug he was careful not to touch me in any manner but a comforting one.

I knew that he had transferred some of his life force to me as encouragement. I knew that it was time to end our student teacher relationship and I wanted him to understand how much he meant to me.

It was the last lesson he gave me and I knew in my soul I would not see him again. We talked for the first time or I talked and he listened. I told him some of the things that I hope to accomplish because I wanted him to understand why I had needed him so much.

When he started to leave I walked to the door with him and I asked him to touch my hair and bless me and to hold me. It did not seem to surprise him.

He rumpled my hair roughly. He grabbed me and held me tight against him. I felt a warmth over the area of my spleen and then a sensation of floating.

That did it, it's not over yet.

I knew it would seem that I was chasing him like a young girl would pursue a lover but I had to go to his church and search for answers. I took Mike to meet the pastor and asked if he would go with me until I could find my answers. He told me it was my story and I needed to go by myself.

I was asking again who Jacob was and how his energy was transferred to me.

The first Sunday no one touched me. The altered state came over me and I knew I was praying in tongues. Something else happened, but like the Prophecy long ago, it was hidden in my subconscious.

The second Sunday no one touched me and I had another overwhelming experience of crying my heart out and not knowing why.

The third Sunday I went down for prayer and as the prayer partners held me I knew I was supposed to be there in waiting. I asked we pray for peace of mind and understanding concerning my book.

The fourth Sunday I went into a class and the lesson was Mark 1:1-6 about the power of Jesus healing the man with the withered hand. It was about the man being in the right place at the right time.

The message I got was that Jacob, whoever he was, had led me to these divine appointments to show me the power.

In the class I freaked out and blurted "What is this power and why is it here in this church?"

We had a lively discussion but the only answer was it is the power of the Holy Spirit and it was there because it was welcome.

Now intellectually I am well read and history and symbol are evidence that even the Bible is just a book of covered messages to a persecuted Hebrew nation.

If there is a Holy Spirit it is because we created it in our own minds.

In creating my story I have imposed on Jacob, suffered rejection and by cracky after all this I am going to come to a conclusion about this energy.

Why was I the messenger that called the churches and church leaders a dead zone? Now why was I being shown a power in a church that is alive with the same power that has overshadowed me and entranced me all my life?

When I started my story I never planned to challenge anyone about anything least of all myself. I just wanted to raise my consciousness. Did I create this personal reality where I had to go through all this year of falling in love, learning computer, Spanish, guitar, video editing and feeling like I was imposing and being rejected just to find my way to this church and the power of light? There is the answer.

Let There Be Light

There is the answer. I have been singing about it in my CD all year. The name of the song is "The Mystery" by Hugin the Bard.

It tells about seekers of light searching the world over only to find they are the light.

I remembered that in two of the books I read about the study of ORMES or elements it had been discovered that there is a zero point light where we all may evolve and use clairvoyance.

They tell us that our aura is a Meissner field where we can make transition to a superconducting state and oscillate at the same frequency or be in resonance with another person.

Our aura or that of another person can be so charged that we would not even have to touch to exchange energy. That is how I have drawn close to the people I have needed at those particular times in my life.

It explains how I can be entrained with a group like the prayers and pain of Jacob's church people.

I must be so sensitive that I tapped into the small group at the church and felt their prayers and pains. It also helped me to know that is the reason I avoid crowds and funerals. It is especially comforting to know that the intense misery I have felt when Mike was angry or shut me out was not as bad as it seemed.

Are we actually at an accelerated time becoming 5th dimensional where our consciousness has been raised enough to be Nibirubian?

Is one of my psychic gifts prophecy where I am foretelling the future of the church leaders?

My daughter in law tells me she does not understand the things I write. I don't completely understand myself and that is why I pray for understanding.

I don't think it matters whether we call it light or Jesus or the Holy Spirit. Whatever it is guides us from within as we program it with our thoughts.

In Jacob's church I found a small group that I tapped into and I believe I found peace of mind and understanding enough to know that at the times I was touched by Jacob we were attuned by our thoughts and that I momentarily became a flash of light.

There is nothing wrong with my imagination.

I would like to end my story now but that is not possible.

Last Sunday the lesson was on Paul's message to the churches and I was given another word of knowledge for the church leaders.

Here at the end of my journey on the social network for the year 2012 I decree:

"Church leaders, covering your behinds will not do any good.
God has seen what you have been doing in secret.
Now live in fear and trembling as you face public humiliation
for it will come."

I am not suffering from inflation of my ego; I am just writing what I hear in my unicameral mind.

From my own premise that I am creating my own personal reality, both the pleasant and the unpleasant, I can see where my actions and reactions could have gone in other directions. In fact it did present some unexpected events. Remembering that I created them made it so much easier to find my way out.

I have never seen more clearly that I have always drawn wonderful people to myself. Some of the actors in my dramas may be a little bewildered at the part I have given them but to all my social network friends old and new I have tried to love and encourage.

I was almost numb and lethargic when I sent out the psychic message for help. Jacob came and brought my thinking back to life. I can almost feel the dendrites in my brain waving and growing.

I finally messaged George and told him that I had learned a lot about human nature this year but I am still the same person he has known for over half his life and I miss him.

He messaged back "Human nature is a stern teacher but friendship is constant." Then he said "Count on mine."

I enter my rest.

Afterword

I wanted to write my story and I wanted to prove to myself that God in me as my effective source would guide me to accomplish this desire of my heart within a year.

I had plenty of blank pages to fill and the stage to envision how to pull together the actors from my past, present and future.

There are several principles that have been at work in me from the time I was very young right up to the present that have kept me on the path of righteousness and contentment even when I was not making good choices.

The first is that I always wanted to know why about everything.

The second is that I hear the voices from the Universe through books and people.

The third is that I believe in magic and the value of myth and enchantment.

The most important guidance I have had came from my mother figures.

Characters

Mike	my husband
Jacob	my computer teacher
Joel	my Spanish teacher
George	my good friend
Drew	my good friend's son